Photo by Jay Thompson
A scene from the Mark Taper Forum production of "Blade to the Heat."
Set design by Yael Pardess.

BLADE TO THE HEAT

BY OLIVER MAYER

Revised Edition

★

DRAMATISTS
PLAY SERVICE
INC.

2

For the Dog

BLADE TO THE HEAT was produced by Mark Taper Forum (Gordon Davidson, Artistic Director; Charles Dillingham, Managing Director) in Los Angeles, California, in April, 1996. It was directed by Ron Link; the set design was by Yael Pardess; the costume design was by Candice Cain; the lighting design was by Anne Militello; the sound design was by Jon Gottlieb; the original musical accompaniment was by East L.A. Taiko; the fight choreography was by Michael Olajidé, Jr.; the production stage manager was James T. McDermott and the stage manager was Mary K Klinger. The cast was as follows:

GARNET .... Hassan El-Amin
THREE-FINGER JACK .... Ellis E. Williams
ALACRAN .... Sal Lopez
MANTEQUILLA DECIMA .... Dominic Hoffman
PEDRO QUINN .... Ray Oriel
REPORTER, ANNOUNCER, REFEREE .... Gerrit Graham
SARITA MALACARA .... Justina Machado
WILFRED VINAL .... Raymond Cruz
ENSEMBLE .... Wayne Brady, César Hernández,
        Maceo Hernandez, Michael Hernandez, Zilah Hill,
        Alfredo Ortiz, William Stephen Taylor, George Villas

BLADE TO THE HEAT was produced by The New York Shakespeare Festival at the Joseph Papp Public Theater (George C. Wolfe, Producer; Jason Steven Cohen, Managing Director) in New York City, in November, 1994. It was directed by George C. Wolfe; the set design was by Riccardo Hernandez; the costume design was by Paul Tazewell; the lighting design was by Paul Gallo; the sound design was by Dan Moses Schreier and the production stage manager was Gwendolyn M. Gilliam. The cast was as follows:

GARNET .... Carlton Wilborn
THREE-FINGER JACK .... Chuck Patterson
ALACRAN .... Jaime Tirelli
MANTEQUILLA DECIMA .... Paul Calderon

4

PEDRO QUINN .... Kamar De Los Reyes
REPORTER, ANNOUNCER, REFEREE .... James Colby
SARITA MALACARA .... Maricela Ochoa
WILFRED VINAL .... Nelson Vasquez

CHARACTERS

PEDRO QUINN
MANTEQUILLA DECIMA
WILFRED VINAL
SARITA
GARNET
THREE-FINGER JACK
ALACRAN
REFEREE/ANNOUNCER/REPORTER

TIME

1959

Only the music. And he swings oh swings;
beyond complete immortal now.

– Robert Hayden

BLADE TO THE HEAT

A bull terrier barking.

Drums.

*Then bell rings. The gym, heavy bags, speed bags, ropes skip-
ping, shoes squeaking. Sweat and cigar smoke. Men working out with each other and in front of mirrors.*

*Then music, loud and strong. Garnet enters, the spitting im-
age of Jackie Wilson. He sings an intense rhythm and blues
number which is strongly imitative of Jackie and of James
Brown. As he sings he executes a tight one-leg shimmy to per-
fection. A moment later, he lands a split, then pulls the mike
close. As the song builds to climax, and he is about to land
the backflip on the downbeat — bell rings. Two fighters spar,
while Three-Finger Jack and Alacran shout instructions.*

JACK.   *(To one.)* The head!
ALACRAN.   *(To the other.) Tira!*
JACK.   Punch him in the head!
ALACRAN.   *El gancho al hígado! Al hígado!*
JACK.   Punch a man in the head it mixes his mind.
ALACRAN.   Work the body! Break him into little pieces! *Tira,
cono! (His man goes down.)* They no listen.
JACK.   Neither did we. We didn't listen to nobody.
ALACRAN.   That's 'cause nobody listened to us!
JACK.   You and me, we was the uncrowned champs.
ALACRAN.   You mean chumps! *(Bell rings. The fighters towel
off, resting. Only Pedro, alone in a corner, continues to shadow-box.)*
JACK.   Yeah, but there's still hope. *(Nodding at Pedro.)* The
boy who wins nowadays got to have the heart, the fire, and
he got to be a roman'ic.

ALACRAN.   Ah, you always talking poetry. *(Cameras flash. Bustle as Mantequilla Decima, the champion, enters with his entourage. Reporter approaches.)*
REPORTER.   Hey Champ! Give us a good shot! *(Mantequilla grins, poses.)* Which hand you gonna knock him out with?
MANTEQUILLA.   *(Brandishing the right hand.)* El Suzie Q.
REPORTER.   Smart money's on you, as always. You beaten everybody else. So what's next? Retire? Run for president? What?
MANTEQUILLA.   I was born to fight. To wear the belt. Is a beautiful sport. A mang can be a mang. You dance, you play, you get angry. But in the end it all come down to *corazón.* And this too. *(Makes a fist.)* My dream? I beat this guy — retire undefeated — then I go home to my country. My people, I love them very much. So after we get rid of this *como-se-llama* Castro, then *quien sabe?*
REPORTER.   You got my vote!
MANTEQUILLA.   Too bad you' not my people! *(Bell rings.)*
ALACRAN.   *(Pointing at Mantequilla, the proud father.)* Que *chulada!* That man is like a god. I useta fight just like that — *egualito!* Decima, he's a trainer's dream, if he gave me a chance, *hijole —!*
JACK.   *(Pointing at Pedro.)* Now that's beautiful. Most beautiful thing in the world, a boy working his little butt off. Pure gold, and you can bet he listens! *(To Pedro, who is boxing.)* Don't burn yerself out now! Take it slow now, 'cause we want you to take that title! Yes we do. Take it on back for all us never got the chance! 'Cause you' our boy!
ALACRAN.   Ain't mine.
JACK.   But he a Messican!
ALACRAN.   With a name like Quinn?
JACK.   Don't blame him, blame his daddy!
ALACRAN.   Mick – Jew – whoever the hell he was.
JACK.   But to go agin yer own —
ALACRAN.   *Y tu, que sabes?* You look in the mirror recently? He ain't black and ugly like you, but he is black!
JACK.   But that don't count, he' a Cuban!
ALACRAN.   Talk trash at me.... Support your own, *cabrón!*

JACK.   Boy like that, you give him half a chance, he' dangerous. Like one of them pit bulls.

ALACRAN.   That mutt? *(Bell rings. Reporter approaches Pedro.)*

REPORTER.   Got anything to say, Kid? *(Pedro takes off his sweats.)* No one expects too much, you going up against the best pound for pound and all that. What do you get from a fight like this? besides a beating? *(Pedro silent.)* Do you really think you can take him?

PEDRO.   Me?

REPORTER.   Yeah you! Who else?

PEDRO.   I'm just gonna do the best I can.

REPORTER.   *(Exiting.)* He's dead! *(Pedro exits the other way.)*

ALACRAN.   *(Looking at Mantequilla.)* There's the man. *Todo hombre. Como esto!* *(Raises his fist like an erection.)*

JACK.   Is that what I think it is? I swear sometimes you' queerer than Dick's hat band.

ALACRAN.   Who?

JACK.   You who!

ALACRAN.   *Tu!*

JACK.   *Tu-tu!* Always knew there was something funny about you, sucka!

ALACRAN.   Who you calling sucka, sucka? *(They slap-box for a few moments, each getting the better of the other, both ending up on the floor.)*

JACK.   *(Winded.)* Damn!

ALACRAN.   *(Winded.)* *Cabrón!*

JACK.   Gonna be a great fight! Two fellas washed in the blood. Just like we was. Two young men with their whole lives ahead of 'em. Two mighty mighty men. Fighting for us. And for that belt. That beautiful belt. Them two — *(Drums.)* They deserve every damn thing they get. *(Bell rings. Cheers, jeers, catcalls. A growing animal hum from an immense crowd. The Ring. Mantequilla and Pedro come to ring center for the fifteenth and final round. The Referee makes them touch gloves. Then they fight. Drums punctuate punches landing or whizzing by. Pedro fights moving forward, throwing punches constantly. Mantequilla retreats boxing beautifully and scoring combinations. Each man scores well and heavily. There's an unintentional head-butt — Referee checks for cuts,*

11

while Pedro apologizes.)

REFEREE. Box! *(Mantequilla lies back, then throws the vaunted Suzie Q — a wide bolo punch which corkscrews up like a machete cutting sugarcane. It lands like a shotgun blast on Pedro's chin. Freeze on what ought to be a knockout — you simply cannot throw a punch any better. Mantequilla steps back, admiring his work. But Pedro absorbs the blow. His body shakes from the impact but he won't fall. Then, inexplicably, he smiles. A mysterious, unsettling smile. Then Pedro drives Mantequilla to the ropes and rains blows. Mantequilla tries to hold, but Pedro yanks himself free. Bell rings. The fight over, they stagger apart. They embrace. Mantequilla confidently does a victory lap around the ring, while Pedro shrouds himself under a towel. The microphone drops from the rafters.)*

ANNOUNCER.   After fifteen rounds.... *(The sound echoes in the stadium.)* We have a split decision.... The winnah, and NEW CHAMPION OF THE WORLD.... PEDRO QUINN!!! QUINN!!! QUINN!!! *(Pandemonium. Cheer, boos. Pedro looks disbelievingly as his hand is raised and the championship belt passes to him. Flashbulbs. Mantequilla alone in defeat. Then music, very Perez Prado.* Dressing room. Mantequilla is unwrapping his hands. The right is hurt. Sarita, in a black turtleneck and pants, lights a cigarette.)*

MANTEQUILLA.   *HIJO de la gran PUTA — !!*

SARITA.   So you lost.

MANTEQUILLA.   *Hijo de la gran PUTA!!! (Flexing the injured hand.) Come mierda — (Hits himself with it.) COME MIERDA!!!*

SARITA.   Don't do that. You're still my champ. Well you are, aren't you? You look good. Not a mark on you. That counts for something. And God knows you dressed better. You won that hands down — he had some very ugly accessories. And the tassels on his shoes. Please. Promise me baby, don't ever wear tassels, tassels went out a long time ago. Lampshades wear tassels, and they're so girly — when you get hit they make you shake like a good-time girl —

MANTEQUILLA.   *Por FAVOR, chica!*

---

* See Special Note on Songs and Recordings on copyright page.

SARITA. So I'm nervous. I never seen you lose.

MANTEQUILLA. I never lose.

SARITA. Everybody loses, baby.

MANTEQUILLA. No' me. I beat them all. *La Havana, Oriente, Ciudad Mexico,* Miami Beach, Estockton, Las Vegas — *las gane todas — con esto — (The left hook.) con el* Suzie Q — *(The right bolo.) y con esto! (Pounds his forehead.)*

SARITA. Yeah, you got a pretty mean headbutt.

MANTEQUILLA. *No, tonta! Mi inteligensia! Mi imaginación!*

SARITA. Just a joke. Little joke —

MANTEQUILLA. *Chicanas.*

SARITA. Don't say that word. I don't like it. Say Spanish.

MANTEQUILLA. *Chicanas!*

SARITA. I'm Spanish! I'm from LA, all right?

MANTEQUILLA. *Como* Quinn?

SARITA. Yeah. Like Quinn. *(Pedro cross the stage. He has a black eye. He looks like a kid. Inexpensive clothes and worn gym bag. Opens a door — camera flashes, screams, shouts of "Peydro" — he reacts as if caught in headlights. Door closes behind him. Meanwhile, Mantequilla strips naked and is about to enter the shower.)* Hurt?

MANTEQUILLA. *(Gestures.)* This hurty.

SARITA. I got a feeling it'll swell back up to size.

MANTEQUILLA. *(Under the spout.)* He no' even punch hard! I hit him goo' *pero* he no wanna go.

SARITA. Us Mexicans are pretty tough.

MANTEQUILLA. Alla time I hit him, he stang there in fronta me, just stang there, *con esa sonrisa comemierda!*

SARITA. He was smiling?

MANTEQUILLA. *(Still showering.)* You no see it?!!!

SARITA. A smile?

MANTEQUILLA. He makey fun of me?!!!

SARITA. My pop always said when you see a guy smiling like you didn't hurt him — you hurt him.

MANTEQUILLA. *Seguro! Sin duda!* I hit him purty goo' *en la panza* — he gonna go hurty when he go pee-pee. He no feel too sexy now.

SARITA. He never did. *(Mantequilla turns off the shower. Advances on her naked.)*

13

MANTEQUILLA. What you say?

SARITA. Dry off baby. We don't want you catching cold. *(Throws him a towel.)* Kinda sexy when you're mad.

MANTEQUILLA. *Oye.* I am always sexy. *(Embraces her.) Que bien te ves, chica.*

SARITA. Just your basic black.

MANTEQUILLA. *Pero* I wish you' wear a dress, *cono!!*

SARITA. They're not beat.

MANTEQUILLA. *Pero* you look like a little boy.

SARITA. That's why you like me. *(He pushes her away.)*

MANTEQUILLA. No play like that! *(He dresses. His clothes are expensive and well-tailored.)*

SARITA. So touchy! Come on. Let's go listen to some jazz. Let's go uptown and dance! A little rum and coke, a lotta me.... You sure you okay?

MANTEQUILLA. *Algo ...*

SARITA. What?

MANTEQUILLA. That guy —

SARITA. Who?

MANTEQUILLA. Quinn!

SARITA. Forget him!

MANTEQUILLA. Too ... *como se dice* ... nice. I no like nice. We fighting, in close, *como esto* — *(Demonstrates on her.)* and I hitting him in *el higado,* in the liver, and he hit me with his head — BOOM! — and he say "Escuse me." Escuse me? What is that? He makey fun of me? I pop this guy — *tremendo golpe como cañonazo* — *y nada. El* Suzie Q — and he just kinda smile. You no see that smile? I gonna see that smile in my dreams! *(Stares at himself in the mirror.)* I gonna see it in my dreams.

SARITA. You hit him so hard I thought you killed him. Some people smile when they die. Maybe he died a little. *(As he dresses in silence.)* You know, I gotta pretty good smile too! You ever dream about my smile?

MANTEQUILLA. No' like that!

SARITA. Well I'm smiling. So forget about Petey Quinn. *(A moment, then.)* Are you hungry — ?

MANTEQUILLA. *Espérate — !*

SARITA. Let's go get something to eat —

MANTEQUILLA. D'you say Petey? Petey Quinn?
SARITA. What do you mean?
MANTEQUILLA. D'you know this guy? This Petey Quinn?
SARITA. Of course I know him!
MANTEQUILLA. *CARAJO!!!*
SARITA. Don't do that.
MANTEQUILLA. D'you go with him?
SARITA. No I didn't go —
MANTEQUILLA. D'YOU WENT WITH HIM?
SARITA. Don't be jealous —
MANTEQUILLA. *COME MIERDA!!!*
SARITA. I don't go out with *Chicanos.* Gimme a little credit here. And DON'T INTERROGATE ME. *(Silence.)* So he's cute. So shoot me.
MANTEQUILLA. CUTE?!!!!
SARITA. I can't even talk about a guy — !!!
MANTEQUILLA. NO OTHER GUYS!!!
SARITA. YOU SEE!!!
MANTEQUILLA. I'm the only guy! I'm the *mang!*
SARITA. Not anymore. *(Silence.)*
MANTEQUILLA. Hmm. *(Collects himself.)* Maybe this time he win. *Pero* the next time — *(Makes fist.)* me llamo Martillo. El *ponchador martillo.* I gonna dead him sure with my hammer.
SARITA. You gonna show him your hammer? I thought I was the only one gets to see it.
MANTEQUILLA. You joke alla time.
SARITA. Not all the time.
MANTEQUILLA. You no like me no more?
SARITA. I like you.
MANTEQUILLA. *Pero,* like that.
SARITA. Yeah, like that. *(They come together, reflected in the mirror.)* Do you ever think about me when you're in the ring? When you're in there, doing what you do, you ever see us making love? *(Kisses his knuckles.)*
MANTEQUILLA. You no make love in the ring.
SARITA. I wish you did. *(Slight pause.)* You look like a champ.
MANTEQUILLA. *Pero* I no champ no more. Chit. Chit chit chit.

SARITA. I love it when you talk dirty.

MANTEQUILLA. I win next time. I get back my belt. I work so hard for that belt!

SARITA. We both do. Let's get beat.

MANTEQUILLA. I no wanna get beat.

SARITA. Not "beat" — Beat. *(A Beat move.)* Red hot and cool.

MANTEQUILLA. Tha's my goo' bad girl. *(Cracks his Sugar Ray Robinson grin.)* I look okay?

SARITA. Baby, you're the champ. *(Music. Classic R & B as Garnet imitates Jackie Wilson and James Brown. The Green Room. Music such as a song by James Brown* playing distantly. Garnet enters, sweating. Pedro is there waiting.)*

GARNET. No stuff! *(They slap five.)* I guess I can call ya Champ. *(Grabs the belt.)* Aw man — I always wanted one of these! *(Walks around with it.)* Local Boy Done Good! *(Resumes undressing.)* I knew you could.

PEDRO. *(Listens to the tune.)* James Brown?

GARNET. The man sweats too much. Can't be healthy. Shouting and wheezing and slaver all over the place. *(Joins him.)* Wish I coulda been there tonight —

PEDRO. Naw, you had a gig —

GARNET. Shoulda took the night off. But I knew you'd win. *(Drinks from flask.)* Here's to the King. And long may he reign. *(Pedro doesn't drink. He seems wound-up, ill at ease. Garnet picks up the championship belt.)* Fit?

PEDRO. Nope.

GARNET. Lemme see.

PEDRO. Didn't think it would be like this.

GARNET. Didn't figure you'd come here. Tonight of all nights. I mean, why ain'tcha out on the town? Must be victory party or something —

PEDRO. I walked out on it.

GARNET. You what?

PEDRO. Didn't feel right.

GARNET. But it was for you!

---

* See Special Note on Songs and Recordings on copyright page.

PEDRO.   I don't want a party. I don't deserve a party.
GARNET.   But you're the Champ! You won —
PEDRO.   It was just a decision. That's no way to beat a king.
GARNET.   *(With the belt.)* But it's yours —
PEDRO.   But it doesn't fit.
GARNET.   Don't they size these things?
PEDRO.   Look. You beat the man who beat the man —
GARNET.   Maybe you're supposed to wear it over one shoulder —
PEDRO.   Like a line of kings. It's supposed to fit. Fit Mantequilla like a glove. He deserved it. He earned it. And now I got it and it just don't fit —
GARNET.   *(Showing him.)* Little clasp on the back.
PEDRO.   He's the Man.
GARNET.   No, you' the Man.
PEDRO.   But —
GARNET.   Don't matter what you think. You' the champ. You passed the test. You come out the other side. *(A new song — such as Jackie Wilson* singing something raucous and gospelly.)* Here. Listen up you damn sad sack. This'll set ya right. This belt will protect you! *(Suddenly Garnet is on his feet lip-synching and dancing to the song, landing a leg-drop, then popping up to a one-leg shimmy. It's wild and sexy and fun.)*
PEDRO.   Wow! You're great!
GARNET.   Not me. Jackie is the king.
PEDRO.   Jackie Wilson?
GARNET.   He's an emperor. But Brown wants the crown.
PEDRO.   They're both kings.
GARNET.   But there's only one crown. *(Slight pause.)* I'd take Jackie any day. Better looking. James just don't look wholesome. Not exactly what you wanna take home to Mom and Pop. Yeah, well neither of them. But see, that's the thing. Don't matter how you look. It's who you are. *(Tousles Pedro's hair.)* You wanna know something? Listen up. James Brown was a boxer.
PEDRO.   Naw!

---

* See Special Note on Songs and Recordings on copyright page.

GARNET. Yep. He boxed. And you know what else? Jackie too.

PEDRO. Jackie boxed? No way.

GARNET. Hey I know some things about boxing too.

PEDRO. But — I mean, he's so cool, — I mean the moves —

GARNET. Those moves of his? Boxing moves. What he learned he learned in the ring. See, he always saved a ringside seat for his Ma. So this one time she doesn't show, and he keeps looking over at the empty seat. So they're grabbing and clutching and leaning on each other and alla sudden Jackie sees her and he can't help himself he just says "Hi Ma!" and — *(Three punches.)* Wop. Bop. Mop. *(Slight pause.)* See, he learned the hard way. Don't be looking to nobody. Not even Mom. Get down to business. And watch yerself in them clinches. Don't wanna get any more than you have to. *(Touches Pedro's eye.)*

PEDRO. Useta dream about fighting Mantequilla. Just shaking his hand — I probably wouldn'ta washed it for a week. Useta dream about it all the time. And then tonight. There I was. Getting smacked around by the Man himself. I had to smile. I was so happy to be there. It made me smile. Even when he really hit me. Weird getting hit. You feel so alive. *(Pause.)* That's the thing.

GARNET. What?

PEDRO. It doesn't last.

GARNET. What doesn't last?

PEDRO. That feeling. That … thing.

GARNET. How's your eye?

PEDRO. I don't feel it.

GARNET. You got to feel something. I mean, you're the champ. You been working your whole life for this! You been dreaming about other guys all these years. Now people gonna start dreaming about you. *(Pedro reacts.)* They will. Probably are already.

PEDRO. But I'm not good enough.

GARNET. *(Clasps his shoulder.)* It's all right. You got what you wished for. It's hard to get what you wish for.

PEDRO. I wish I could be like you.

GARNET.   You don't wanna be like me.

PEDRO.   And do what you do onstage. And move like that —

GARNET.   Like what?

PEDRO.   Like that move. You know — the one, the one —

GARNET.   It's a tough one, you gotta keep your concentration. I studied Jackie like a book, worked on it for days and days in fronta the mirror. You gotta look super-sharp, you gotta look the people in the eye, you gotta be able to top all the knee-drops and one-leg shimmies them other contenders be putting up, you gotta be right in the middle of the song when they're right in the palm of your hand, when it's all on the line, and you gotta *(Demonstrates.)* land that backflip on the downbeat, come right on back with a shooby-doo-wop, and your pompadour not even mussed! Yeah, I nailed it. *(They slap five on the blackhand side.)*

PEDRO.   I've spent my whole life in fronta the mirror, and I never been that good. I never been there. If I could be like you, and not get hit —

GARNET.   Oh I get hit. Every damn day of my life. Half the time they're talking through my set. Bust my gut, they don't give a good goddamn — *(Hi-fi plays a new 45 — something like a classic Jackie Wilson.*)*

PEDRO.   He's the king. *(Sings along tentatively.)* Help me out, wouldya?

GARNET.   Naw, this ain't my key. *(He gives in, sings a bit, then breaks off.)* Nuh-uh. Can't touch that. Too good. *(A moment, then.)*

PEDRO.   I better go.

GARNET.   Lemme see you with the belt on.

PEDRO.   No I can't. I don't wanna — *(From the back, Garnet puts the belt around Pedro. Each backs away.)* What? Does it look dumb? Is it that bad?

GARNET.   It's beautiful.

PEDRO.   It's what?

GARNET.   You the man. No more doggin' around. *(Drums.*

---

* See Special Note on Songs and Recordings on copyright page.

The gym. Spot on Wilfred Vinal as he hits the heavy bag — also curses, sweet-talks, even dry-fucks it. Jack and Alacran watch.)

JACK.   Boy got more tricks than a hooker. And just as cheap.

ALACRAN.   That's *El Chapo* Vinal. He's famous! He's from New York City! He's in the top ten.

JACK.   Top ten?!! Top-ten what? Public Enemies? You gotta be kidding —

ALACRAN.   He's better than he looks. He come out here to fight Mantequilla and the weiner gets your boy — Quinn. For the title.

JACK.   I'll be doggone. *(As Vinal exits.)* Oh man! He' a tomato can!

ALACRAN.   So Mantequilla crush the tomato can, make a little salsa. Then he get the rematch *con* Quinn, and this time'll be different. This time we find out who's the better man. Who's the real champ around here. *(Spits.)* Quinn? *Chingao! Cabrón* think he's too good for us! We throw him a victory party, he hardly even show up! What? Something wrong with us? We ain't good enough? Little bastid got no respect — !

JACK.   You just sore 'cause he beat the flies offa your boy Mantequilla.

ALACRAN.   *Watchale, amigo.* Decima will be king again. *(Drums.)* Vinal first. Then Quinn. *(The arena. The tenth and final round. Mantequilla and Vinal at ring center. Bell rings. Mantequilla stalks Vinal, who thrusts, grabs, and clinches. To the beat of the drums, he makes a ballet out of fouling. Referee cautions him.)*

REFEREE.   Watch the elbows!

VINAL.   *(To Mantequilla.)* Watch the elbows!

REFEREE.   *(Pointing at Vinal.)* You! *(Mantequilla attacks — Vinal sidesteps, then punches him in the ass. They trade viciously. Vinal fouls him, then clinches.)*

VINAL.   Don't clinch me baby, I don't do no bendover.

REFEREE.   You two wanna dance, do it in the dark!

VINAL.   What are you, some kinda faggot? *(Vinal blows him a kiss from a safe distance. Enraged, Mantequilla crushes him with right hand, then punishes him in perfect rhythm with the drums. Vinal in trouble on the ropes as Mantequilla sets him up for the coup de grace — the Suzie Q. Vinal goes down. Takes the eight count.*

Rising, Mantequilla flurries and Vinal goes down hard. The Referee stops the contest.) What're you doing?!! Don't walk away from me — *(Mantequilla raises his gloves in victory. Vinal nearly hits the Referee, who exits fast.)* How could you stop it?!!! I wasn't hurt. I had him right where I wanted him! I was gonna knock him out! I had him! I had him right here in the palm of my hand! *(Commotion in the ring. Vinal plays the crowd.)*

ANNOUNCER.   *(As microphone drops from the rafters.)* The winnah, by knockout, Mantequilla Decima — !! *(Mantequilla raises his glove. Vinal throws a tantrum. Into the microphone:)*

VINAL.   Decima!! That faggot? He din't knock me out! You give it to that faggot? You can't give it to that faggot! No, you can't give it to that faggot — !

MANTEQUILLA.   Faggot?

VINAL.   Faggot! *Tu* baby! Let that little fag kick your ass. Fucking Pedro Queen! Ain't no fag ever gonna beat me — *(Rhythmic, a chant.)* Come on, say it with me! *Ma-ri-cón! Ma-ri-cón! (As Vinal continues to chant in and out of the ring, TV Reporter and cameraman approach.)*

TV REPORTER.   *(On the move.)* ... the ex-champion definitely had the high-spirited New Yorker in trouble on the ropes ... *(Sidles up to Mantequilla.)* Here we are with the victor, Mantequilla Decima, in a bit of a wild scene. Were you bothered by Vinal's tactics?

MANTEQUILLA.   Huh?

TV REPORTER.   Tactics. He seemed to be talking to you during the contest. What was he saying? Was he trying to tell you something? I'm sure our viewers at home would be very interested to hear — Like the word he's saying now. Marigold? Perhaps you could translate. Go ahead, give us the gist if you c — *(Mantequilla grabs the mike.)*

MANTEQUILLA.   I win this fight no problem, *pero* I no rest till I get *la revancha con* Quinn.

TV REPORTER.   *(Adjusting his toupee.)* You want to fight Pete Quinn again?

MANTEQUILLA.   I want to fight Quinn. I prove I am a real mang. I dead him. I promise.

ANNOUNCER.   Well, there you have it! And just remember

you heard it first on —

VINAL. *(Grabbing the mike away from him.)* He di'nt beat me! He's a fag! They're all fags! And Pete Quinn, he's the biggest fag of all!

ANNOUNCER. Cut it for chrissakes!

VINAL. *(Into camera.)* Hi Mami. *(Drums and music, mixed with the ongoing chant of "Ma-ri-cón" give way to the sounds of the gym. Pedro skips rope. Alacran and Jack watch from a distance.)*

ALACRAN. *Mira, cabrón!*

JACK. What am I looking at?

ALACRAN. See? There!

JACK. Where? Man, I don't believe it.

ALACRAN. The way he moves. Look! That little sashay.

JACK. Man, if that's a sashay —

ALACRAN. It's right there in fronta your face — *(Bell rings.)*

JACK. Say Champ!

PEDRO. Say Jack.

JACK. How ya feel?

PEDRO. I feel good.

JACK. You catch Mantequilla and Vinal? They stunk up the joint pretty bad. They didn't show me nothing. I think you got their number.

PEDRO. Don't jinx me. *(Each knocks wood.)*

JACK. I gotta admit, I wasn't sure we was gonna beat him, you being the unknown commodity and all that. But I like the way you do business. Real straight up. You done us proud.

PEDRO. Thanks, Jack. *(They shake, boxer-style.)*

ALACRAN. Say Champ.

PEDRO. Alacran.

ALACRAN. *Como esta la novia?*

PEDRO. Huh?

ALACRAN. *La novia.* What? You no speaka Spanish? Your girlfriend. How's she doing?

PEDRO. Don't got one.

ALACRAN. Que no! There's gotta be somebody. Come on! You can tell me. *Te gusta meter mano?*

PEDRO. Huh?

ALACRAN. *Meter mano?* Well. Ain't that a shame. Young fella like you and no *panocha* to be had. Don't you like a little tail between fights? After all, you the Man —

JACK.   *(Getting between them.)* Don't mind him, Champ. He don't know nothing, wetback always talking out his ass. *(Bell rings. Pedro resumes the workout.)* What the fuck you doing?

ALACRAN.   I'm tryna show you something!

JACK.   You mammyjamming old buzzard. You punch-drunk or what?

ALACRAN.   You don't believe me? Are you blind?

JACK.   I wish I was deaf — *(Garnet enters. Alacran and Jack instinctively form a human wall between him and Pedro.)* Can I help you?

ALACRAN.   You got business?

GARNET.   Um ... I'll come back another time — *(About to exit.)*

PEDRO.   Hey! It's okay. Let him through. He's with me. *(Jack moves aside, but Alacran doesn't budge. Garnet slides past him with a dance move.)* Make yourself at home. *(Garnet does another tight dance step.)* Wow! What was that?

GARNET.   You ain't the only one been working hard. I'm breaking in a new song tonight at the club.

PEDRO.   Jackie? James?

GARNET.   Just me. Been waiting a long time. Now it's my time. No more impersonating. *(Alacran shadows him.)*

PEDRO.   Cool.

GARNET.   *(Looking around.)* So this is it.

PEDRO.   Not like the movies, huh?

GARNET.   Place could use a good clean. *(Alacran slams a locker shut.)* Where is everybody?

PEDRO.   *(Shrugs.)* I prefer the quiet.

GARNET.   *(As Alacran continues to shadow him.)* I'ma go —

PEDRO.   No! I mean, it's okay. I never had a friend come up before.

GARNET.   Hey, you the champ, you got a million friends. *(Alacran scoffs.)* Well there's a line of teenyboppers down the block waiting to get a look at the new champ.

PEDRO.   I wish!

GARNET.   You look good. *(Alacran whistles.)* Here, I mean.

PEDRO.   It's what I know. *(Bell rings.)*

GARNET.   *(Awkward.)* Pedro. Be at the club tonight?

PEDRO.   I'll be there.

GARNET.   All right. *(Garnet exits quickly. Pedro works the heavy bag for a moment. Then looks up.)*

PEDRO.   That's my friend! *(Resumes workout.)*

ALACRAN.   You see? You see?

JACK.   What? It's a friend, ya damn fool! What's wrong with that?

ALACRAN.   I knew it. It's what I told you, except it's worse! Fucking little *Chicano* bastid! He's pissing on us. On the belt. On the game. On us. You shoulda listened to me.

JACK.   You get outa his business.

ALACRAN.   It's our business.

JACK.   What the hell's it got to do with you?

ALACRAN.   Everything, Jack. Every goddamn thing.

JACK.   That boy deserves respect!

ALACRAN.   Respect my ass!

JACK.   Goddamn gossip! You're like some old woman! I'm sick of it —

ALACRAN.   Now this is what we do. Cut him off. No talk. No warning. Just cut him off.

JACK.   But he' my boy — !

ALACRAN.   Not if you know what's good for you. *(Silence.)* So. You with me?

JACK.   Respect!

ALACRAN.   Don't walk away from me!

JACK.   *(To Pedro.)* I'll hold the bag for ya, Champ.

ALACRAN.   What you get angry with me for? He's the one! HE'S THE MARICÓN!!! *(Pedro freezes. Feels all eyes on him. Then resumes hitting the bag one blow at a time.)*

JACK.   That's it boy.... Stay within yourself.... Don't pay that fool no never mind.... That's it! *(Pedro wears himself out on the bag.)*

ALACRAN.   *(Laughs at him.)* He don't even deny it. He knows who he is! CUT HIM OFF!!! *(Drums. Mambo. Cuban flags. Airport tarmac. Mantequilla enters dancing with Sarita to the hottest sexiest mambo you have ever seen. Both of them dripping with style. They*

24

finish to applause. He addresses a crowd.)
MANTEQUILLA.   I bery bery glad to be here in Miami. And
to the *Cubanos* who are here, *le quiero decir que viva Cuba! Que
Viva Cuba Libre!*
SARITA.   Give us room please!
REPORTER.   Say Champ, the word was you were gonna re-
tire before ya got beat. Care to comment? *(He doesn't.)* Aren't
you getting a little too old for the game?
MANTEQUILLA.   *(Smiling through anger.)* I gonna be champ
again real soon.
REPORTER.   What about Quinn?
SARITA.   What about him?
REPORTER.   What about all this stuff coming from Wilfred
Vinal?
MANTEQUILLA.   Vinal? *Un imbécil. Pero* he taught me some-
thing.
REPORTER.   You mean it's true?
SARITA.   *Payaso!* He just told you —
MANTEQUILLA.   *Cálmate*, baby. *(They kiss, very sexy and public.)*
SARITA.   He's all man! You see? You see? *(Grabs his arm.)*
Get a picture. *(Camera flash.)*
MANTEQUILLA.   We no' married yet, but we will be soon.
(Motions for silence.) Soy todo hombre. Todo hombre! That's why I
gonna win. You no can win *si es afeminado — como se dice —
un* FAGGOT, *un maricón.* Vinal, he teach me you can no' trust
the other guy. The other guy can be a bad mang. Or no mang
at all. Now I have no mercy. Just like these beautiful Cuban
people gonna have no mercy for *los malos Communistas!
Revolucion? Mierda! Buncha maricón drogadictos, hijos de la gran
puta que se llama Comunismo. Castro?! Guevara?!* Who are these
guys? Get a shave! Put on some decent clothes! Then talk to
me. Freedom fighters? *Aquí estamos!* The real freedom fighters.
And me, I yam a freedom fighter! I fight for the goo' people
— the normal people — of these beautiful *Estados Unidos!* How
can I lose? *(Applause, the million-dollar grin.)* T'ank you. *(Chants
of "Ma-ri-cón" mixed with drums. Terrorizing nightmare sounds mixed
with way-out jazz. As in a bad dream, images float past in darkness.
Two fighters, their faces obscured, are grabbing and clutching each*

other. The Referee appears.)

REFEREE.   I keep having this dream. I'm in there working, but it's like I'm in molasses, I can hardly move. And the fighters, well they're just teeing off. Not just punches, I'm talking headbutts and elbows and laces and there's blood everywhere. I know I oughta stop it, I mean hell, everybody knows, they're screaming at me. I feel like screaming too, but I got the cotton mouth, can't get nothing out. And it's getting bad. The one fella, well he's just getting ruint. Finally I get the feeling back, I can move, I can stop this thing. But the thing is, I don't. I let it go. I just let it go. *(The fighters continue, more like they're fucking than fighting. Drums intensify. The fighters disappear as Mantequilla wakes from the dream. Sarita beside him. They are alone in bed.)*

MANTEQUILLA.   *NO LO SOY!!!!*

SARITA.   What?

MANTEQUILLA.   *No lo soy.*

SARITA.   What are you talking about?

MANTEQUILLA.   *Por que maricón?*

SARITA.   I don't know.

MANTEQUILLA.   *Por que?!!*

SARITA.   Dammit!!

MANTEQUILLA.   *Dime!!! Por que?!!!*

SARITA.   NOT YOU!!! *(Silence.)*

MANTEQUILLA.   Quinn?

SARITA.   Look, it's not true.

MANTEQUILLA.   How you know?

SARITA.   We went to school together. High school! They put all the Mexican kids in the same school —

MANTEQUILLA.   D'YOU WENT WITH HIM?!!!

SARITA.   You gotta be kidding! He's from El Monte, wrong side of the tracks. I'm from Montebello, we know these things. *(He stares at her.)* He wouldn't go out with me, okay? You satisfied?

MANTEQUILLA.   He no go out with you?

SARITA.   No he no go out with me. That bastard Vinal. He was just messing with your mind. He was just trying to hurt you, to make you mad, make you crazy —

MANTEQUILLA.   Oh no. *(Slaps himself.)*
SARITA.   What?
MANTEQUILLA.   I lose to a...? No no no. *(Slaps himself.)*
SARITA.   Don't do that!
MANTEQUILLA.   *No me toques!* Everybody know. Now I know.
SARITA.   Nobody knows anything! I mean, come on! This is
the Fifties! What's the problem —
MANTEQUILLA.   *(Grabbing her.)* No lie. This Quinn — this
Petey — *es macho o no es mucho?* No lie. This cute guy. Did
he...? *Contigo...? (Gestures lewdly.) Que paso, baby? Que paso — ?*
SARITA.   NOTHING! We did nothing! *(He lets her go.)*
MANTEQUILLA.   Then he is. *(Drums. Mantequilla grabs his
pants and gym bag and exits in a rush. Lights, live music intro.)*
GARNET.   *(Onstage at the club.)* I'd like to do something different and dedicate this to a special friend. *(Then Garnet
launches into song. The ideal rhythm and blues version of a song
such as a Piaf standard,* but sung in his own voice. Garnet hits
the high notes as best he can — no imitation, just him — we can
tell how much it means to him. He sounds great, but the crowd boos
him off the stage. Down and dirty stripjoint sax in the distance. Pedro
finds him in the Green Room.)*
PEDRO.   You were great!
GARNET.   Muthafuckas!
PEDRO.   No, you were great.
GARNET.   Two-bit bastids —
PEDRO.   You'll get another gig —
GARNET.   I was good!
PEDRO.   A better gig!
GARNET.   They wouldn't know talent if it kicked 'em in the
ass.
PEDRO.   You could even play the Apollo Theater —
GARNET.   You gotta be kidding.
PEDRO.   I was just tryna —
GARNET.   Well don't. Don't be so got-damn positive about
me. When I sang that song, the Boss said "What the fuck is
that? Who the hell you think you are? Josephine Baker? Some

* See Special Note on Songs and Recordings on copyright page.

27

piece of French toast? You think we wanna hear you? See you? Singing in French? Singing in your own sorry-ass voice? What the fuck is that?" And he fired me. And he was right. *(Silence.)* There won't be any more gigs.

PEDRO.   But —

GARNET.   Look. I'm an impersonator. Get that in your head, please. I fake Jackie Wilson. I fake James Brown. I shoulda known. Nobody wants to hear me. That's the way it is. That's who the hell I am. And that's it.

PEDRO.   But — *(Struggles with the words.)* That's the thing. You don't have to be yourself. *(Silence.)* The rest of us, we gotta be ourselves all the time.

GARNET.   You're not getting it —

PEDRO.   I got it. I felt it when you sang. When you moved. That — thing. You got it, man. You hit me right between the eyes. You knock me out.

GARNET.   But you're not getting —

PEDRO.   You. *(They're close together. Garnet looks at Pedro conflicted — confused, flattered — not sure what to say.)*

GARNET.   So what do we do now?

PEDRO.   We do the best we can. *(Drums. Mantequilla at the gym on the heavy bag. With each blow he sends it swinging. Alacran watches.)*

ALACRAN.   You look beautiful! *Como chocolate! Que lindo eres!* *(Mantequilla suffers his attentions with some embarassment. Bell rings.)* Precioso! Chingonazo! You look like a fucking god! That little half-breed *pendejo* — ! *(Spits.)* He's dead! *(Turns confidential.)* Listen *m'hijo* — *Quiero hablar contigo* — I need to talk to you — *(Sarita appears. Tension in the room. Long pause.)*

SARITA.   Hey. I figured you oughta get the lay of the land. So here I am.

ALACRAN.   *Pinche's rucas!* It ain't like I don't like girls, I like 'em fine. *Pero en la cocina con una pata rota.* *(The men laugh.)*

SARITA.   In the kitchen with a broken leg? Is that how you want me?

ALACRAN.   Come on, *mamacita*, it was a joke —

SARITA.   Who the hell are you, Cantinflas? *(To Mantequilla.)* Is that how you want me? *(Thrusts her leg out.)* Then break it.

I'll call you when dinner's ready.

MANTEQUILLA. *Siempre con las bromas. (Bangs the bag hard.)* No more jokes.

SARITA. Who's joking?

ALACRAN. I thought it was purty funny.

MANTEQUILLA. *(Suddenly dangerous, commanding.)* You shut up, okay? *Pa' fuera!* Get outa here! *(Alacran leaves, hurt.)* What the hell you doing here?

SARITA. What am I supposed to do?

MANTEQUILLA. No come to the gym no more. *Por favor.* Is hard ... *es duro.*

SARITA. You no like me no more?

MANTEQUILLA. I got to stay clean! I got to beat this guy! This Quinn! Is my last chance!

SARITA. What? You see me you gotta lay me right here? In the ring? Not a bad idea.

MANTEQUILLA. I got to be strong!

SARITA. I love you.

MANTEQUILLA. I no wanna lose!

SARITA. Nobody's gonna lose. *(She approaches, taking off items of clothes. He tries to back away.)* Baby ...

MANTEQUILLA. No, *chica* —

SARITA. No more losing —

MANTEQUILLA. *Por favor, no* —

SARITA. It'll be okay. You fight better when you're relaxed — *(She touches him. He reacts as if from electric shock.)*

MANTEQUILLA. No, *cono!!!*

SARITA. I know you. If you hold it in too long, you'll explode — *(She has both hands on him. By now he's caving in.)*

MANTEQUILLA. *Ay yi yi* —

SARITA. And you know me, I'll explode —

MANTEQUILLA. *Ay no.*

SARITA. Yes.

MANTEQUILLA. Please.

SARITA. I'll handle everything. *(They grab each other like hungry animals. She goes to her knees.)* You're beautiful — *(In his head, he hears the chant of Ma-ri-cón.)* You're the champ — *(He backs away in pain.)*

MANTEQUILLA. *NO LO SOY!!! (Exits.)*

SARITA. *(Exiting after him.)* You're not gonna cut me off!!!
(Drums. Flashbulbs. Vinal jumps rope wildly, masterfully. A display of utter ballet and contained violence. Reporter watches.)

REPORTER. So who you gonna call a fag today?

VINAL. You. *(Unsure laughter.)* I tell it like it is. *(Takes the speed bag.)* See that? That's Pete Quinn's little head. And this is what I'm gonna do to it. *(Bangs it.)* Little half-breed *cholo* bastid — *(Bangs it.)* I ain't no mixed blood. *Yo soy boriqua! Puro sangre.* I gots the blood of some kick-ass cannibals in these veins. *(Displays forearm.)* See that? That's Indio, baby. *El Carib.* Quinn fucks with me, I'ma stick him in a pot and make chicken soup.

REPORTER. You wanna fight Pete Quinn?

VINAL. You want me to fuck him instead? Sure! Mantequilla don't deserve no rematch! Gimme the fight. I'll show the world. I'll tell you this. I better not bump into him in no men's room, 'cause my papi told me don't stand for no *patitos.*

REPORTER. *(Writing in his notepad.)* Potatoes?

VINAL. You want the truth, you come to me. Straight up no chaser.

REPORTER. You use me, I use you.

VINAL. Come back tomorrow for some more. Okay?

REPORTER. *(Exiting.)* Okay.

VINAL/REPORTER. Loser. *(Jack enters.)*

VINAL. No autographs.

JACK. I don't want your chicken-scratch!

VINAL. Then beat it, old man!

JACK. They call me Three-Finger Jack —

VINAL. You got all five fingers, you old bastard —

JACK. Course I do. I'm tough but I ain't stupid!

VINAL. Listen Tough Guy. I ain't got time —

JACK. Neither do I. So how do you know?

VINAL. Know what?

JACK. You don't, do ya. Don't know a got-damn thing.

VINAL. You gone punchy?

JACK. You ain't good enough to shine Pete's shoes. I bet you' the freaky-deaky one. *(Walks away.)*

VINAL.   What'd you call me — *(Vinal spins him around. Jack turns fists raised. Vinal cracks up laughing.)* You guys from LA are crazy!

JACK.   You got any idea what you done to that boy?

VINAL.   You mean that *mariconcito* — ?

JACK.   How the hell would you know?

VINAL.   It's obvious, man. You can see it a mile away.

JACK.   I don't see nothing.

VINAL.   You prob'ly ain't got a hard-on in ten years. What's it matter anyway?

JACK.   You don't SAY that, not in this line of business. You KNOW that. You tryna destroy him? Somebody put you up to it? Why, you damn fool, why?

VINAL.   Look, you in the ring with a dude, you get to know him all kinda ways. Like if he eats garlic, or goes heavy on the greasy kid stuff, or if he don't wash under the arms so good. You get to know these things. You was a fighter, you know this. Gimme a little credit here.

JACK.   What, he had a hard-on, what?

VINAL.   You come to a stinky gym like this for a reason. It's always something. Some assholes they just like to fight. Other guys they got to prove something. The little ones they got a complex. Big ones they got a complex too. Some of these clowns like to beat on other guys to impress the chicks, like it'll make their dick bigger or something. Then there's the other kind. They here 'cause they like the smell of men. They like to share sweat. They like the form, man. The way a dude looks when he throws a blow, his muscles all strained and sweaty, his ass all tight bearing down on the blow, his mouth all stopped up with a piece of rubber, and only a pair of soaking wet trunks between his johnson and yours. They like it. And they like to catch a whupping for liking it. That's just the way it is. I'm surprised, man. Thought you knew the business, oldtimer.

JACK.   You don't got a shred of evidence.

VINAL.   What do you want? Pictures? Come on! I'd fuck him! I'd fuck you.

JACK.   You' sick.

VINAL.   I tell it like it is. If some dude wants to go down on me, bring him on! I'll fuck anything! But ain't nobody fucking me, I draw the line, baby! *(Jack pushes him.)* Hey, what's that for — *(Jack pushes him again.)* Look old man — *(Again.)* I'm warning you — !

JACK.   Of course I know what goes on. Been going on since the beginning of time. So what. You gotta go wreck a man's life?

VINAL.   It worked, didn't it?

JACK.   I oughta kick your ass.

VINAL.   You go for the other guy's weakness, right? Am I right? He got a cut eye, you gonna hit him in the elbow? Come on! You jam your glove in there, you rip the fucker open. Tell me I'm wrong. *(Silence.)* When I fought Decima, that piece of trash called my *mamita* some dirty-ass names. I got mad. I din't fight so good. Okay, he found my weakness. I can live with that. I love my *mami*. But I vowed to God I'd get him back one way or the other. That's how I turned the fight around. All it takes is a single word. Hey, one look at him and I knew that macho crap would make him go crazy. Guy like that is stupid enough to think we really care where he sticks his two-incher. He ain't so great as everybody thinks. So, a little word, I got his mind messed up. And then I kicked his ass! I shoulda got that decision too! I wuz robbed, baby! I wuz robbed! *(Slight pause.)* But the guy to worry about is Decima, not Quinn. Quinn is what he is. But I'll bet Decima is a little confused.

JACK.   You got it all figured out.

VINAL.   I'm a student of the game.

JACK.   This ain't what the game's about.

VINAL.   Nothing's about anything.

JACK.   Take it back. Get the TV people. Tell them what you told me.

VINAL.   Fuck that.

JACK.   It ain't too late!

VINAL.   Come off it, old man. Only need to say that kinda shit once. It sticks. Like glue. Like a cheap suit. Hey man. It's business. You talk to me when I'm champ, maybe I'll throw a few bucks your way.... If you bend over. *(Blows Jack a kiss.)* So long, *maricón. (Exits.)*

JACK. I shoulda KICKED his ass! *(Drums. Extreme light change. Alacran joins Jack. They strip to their undershirts. They assume fighting poses.)*

ALACRAN. *Le diera partido en la madre! (The Referee moves in and out, as if working a fight. Crowd noise punctuates their stories. They speak to us in a place outside time.)*

JACK. Back in my prime, be like taking candy from a baby! Hell, I'da been champ if they'da let me!

ALACRAN. *Yo Tambien! Chingao!*

JACK. But they wouldn't fight us.

ALACRAN. *Pinches* white boys.

JACK. Dempsey wouldn't fight colored!

ALACRAN. Woulda kicked his ass!

JACK. Woulda knocked the flies offa that cheating lug! Only reason he hit so hard was he had a roll of nickels in his glove — see, white folk are like that.

ALACRAN. Colored too. And I got the scars to prove it. *Esto? (His hand.) Un* sparring session *con un negrito de* Detroit name of Ray Robinson. He come out here *para pelear con* Baby Arizmendi. He wanna spar *con Mejicanos.* So they get me, dollar a day. They call him The Dancing Man. Well, that's all he did, dance! *Pero* I watching him, I watching him alla time. I cut off the ring, he dance right to me, I catch him on the ropes and — POW! — *la izquierda, y* — WOP! — *un derechazo como relampago!* Now he dancing all right, *pero* like he drunk or something! End of the round, nigger in a suit come up to me gimme ten bucks and tell me to get out.

REFEREE. Punch and get out!

ALACRAN. Ray Robinson? I coulda taken that *pinche comose-llama* any day. Din't even know my hand was broke.

JACK. This? *(Runs a finger across his brow.)* This one I got first time I fought at the Hollywood Stadium. Richie Lemos. I was hot outa Cleveland, they sent me out here to whup me some Messicans. Only Messicans I ever seen was doing stoop labor out fronta the white folks' house. At the weigh-in the greaser he outweighs me eight pounds. Shoulda backed out right there, but I was a damn-fool youngblood, I said "Bring him on" — *(Bell.)*

REFEREE. *(Finishing the ten-count.)* Yer out!

JACK. He kicked my ass.

REFEREE. I'm doing a fight down in San Diego 'bout fifteen years back. Joe Louis on the Bum of the Month tour. All white fellas and he's knocking 'em out right and left. Lemme tell ya, that was one powerful colored man, made people nervous. So just before the fight, this old geezer comes up. One eye is off and he's a weird-looking sonofabitch. Baggy plaid pants and a red tie, and his hair greased on the sides and shaped like devil horns, and he's making like this — *(Extending pinkies and forefingers.)* And he's screaming Cockadoodle doo! Cockadoodle doo!

ALACRAN. *Lo estaba embrujando.*

JACK. Making some whammy.

REFEREE. He was putting the whammy on Ol' Cotton Eye Joe. And Joe didn't much like it neither. See, fighters is like kids. They believe in all that bunk. Especially them black and latin types. Somebody figured the old bastard might get under Joe's skin, spook 'im, you know, give the Bum a chance to send Joe back to the cotton fields.

ALACRAN. Hey, you get any edge you can.

JACK. But it cuts both ways.

REFEREE. So King Joe comes out and puts the Bum to sleep in no time flat. Didn't wanna be in that ring any longer than he had to. Walked right outa that arena, didn't even take a shower. Left town before you could say Jack Robinson. Whammies and cockadoodle doos. Maybe that's why they call 'em spooks. That's the fights for ya. *(Exits.)*

JACK. We was jinxed. But it'a be different for Pete —

ALACRAN. It'a be different for Mantequilla —

JACK. They gonna RESPECT us!

ALACRAN. They gonna give us what we deserve!

JACK. *(Confronts the audience.)* You hear me? RESPECT. You are gonna respect us.

ALACRAN. *O le diera dado en la madre! a la chingada!*

REFEREE. Come on! Pick it up! What the hell you think

this is?

JACK/ALACRAN.   It's a fight. *(Light change. Drums give way to mariachi music. Alacran joins Mantequilla in a seedy Mexican bar. Renderings of boxers from yesteryear on the walls.)*

ALACRAN.   *Te gusta?* Purty good, no? *(Looks around.)* Boxeadores Mejicanos, Cubanos — Latinos — *los mejores del mundo.* They got you over there. Looking good. I useta have my pitcher here too, *alla — Campeon nacional de Mexico.* I was Number Two in the World for a whole year. *Hombre,* I useta get free drinks alla time. *Cabrones.* Can you believe it? I come in here, they painted it over. Put up some little *mayate,* little black guy *comemierda —*

MANTEQUILLA.   Sugar Ray Robinson?

ALACRAN.   Yeah, that's the guy. *(Toasts.)* Arriba, abajo ... *cualquiera.* Here's to the real champ.

MANTEQUILLA.   *Oye, viejo.* Tell me what you got to tell me.

ALACRAN.   Pero I got so much. *Información.* I got *tácticas.* I know how to beat Quinn.

MANTEQUILLA.   I know how.

ALACRAN.   *Pues si!* You're the better man. The moves are sweet, and that right hand of yours is just like a machete. Two years ago you'da cut him down like a buncha sugar cane.

MANTEQUILLA.   *(Bristling.)* Two years ago?

ALACRAN.   Hey, it happens to everybody.

MANTEQUILLA.   I gonna be champ again — !

ALACRAN.   Sure!

MANTEQUILLA.   I gonna get him! Dyou hear me? I gonna dead him —

ALACRAN.   Sure you will. But different. You gonna get him with *tácticas. (Drinks.)* I been watching him. I know how to break him down. You got to find the angles. You got to make him think. About himself. Start by going downstairs.

MANTEQUILLA.   It no work last time.

ALACRAN.   *(Indicating the groin.)* I'm talking low. *Le tienes que romper las bolas. Los putos huevos.*

MANTEQUILLA.   I no fight dirty!

ALACRAN.   Not dirty! *Tácticas. Tu sabes?* TEATRO. *(Silence.)* 'Cause Pedro Quinn he don't know nothing about *teatro.* That

35

boy don't got no sense of humor. He can be taken. No sense of humor.

MANTEQUILLA.   Then how come he smile at me?

ALACRAN.   Huh?

MANTEQUILLA.   He laughing at me! How come he laughing at me?!!!

ALACRAN.   Laughing? He just looking at you like you' something good to eat. He prob'ly got the hots for you. Can't wait to clinch you! That's as close as he gets to you know what! That's what I'm telling you! Don't fight this guy straight on. Play with him. Make him think one thing — *(Leaps in suddenly with a punch.)* Then do the other. BOOM. *El Martillo. El* Suzie Q. *El Campeon. (Drinks.) Teatro. (Both are quiet, awkward.) Hey, es que,* I'm your *compadre.* I'm doing this as a friend. I'm doing this for *La Raza.* In my day, Quinn he'd be dead. You get to be my age, you know what's right and what's wrong. Nobody got to tell you. You just know. I mean, the little shit can't even speak Spanish! Don't even speak his own language! Too many *cabrones* like that running around these days, breaking all the traditions. No respect! Don't know who the hell they are. That's what's wrong. He ain't pure.

MANTEQUILLA.   Pure nothing is pure.

ALACRAN.   The way we feel about you, that's pure. That's real. That's how come you got to win for us. We love you, son. We love you to death. *(He embraces Mantequilla too hard and for too long. When there is no response of affection, he pulls away.)* Hey. *Cabrón* like me sticks around the gym as long as me, he must have some kinda reason, no? He must be good for something. Not like I'm some kinda stiff, some kinda *pinche* has-been.... They forget.... I was Number Two in the World for a whole year — *(Breaks off. Suddenly like a little boy.)* But it ain't like I'm asking for nothing ... *(Mantequilla about to exit. Looks at Alacran awhile.)*

MANTEQUILLA.   *Oye.* You come. You work my corner.

ALACRAN.   You mean it? *(Mantequilla nods, exits.) Teatro. (Drums. Garnet and Pedro together, alone.)*

GARNET.   Useta be like that. Like you. Getting smacked around. Fighting all the time, fighting myself. I had to fight to find the music, I had to fight. That's why you gotta stay focused, man. That's why you gotta keep your head. That's why you gotta be who you are —

PEDRO. You ever had a dog?

GARNET. Say what?

PEDRO. Have you ever had a dog?

GARNET. Been bit too many times.

PEDRO. Had a bull terrier.

GARNET. Got bit by one of those. Muthafuckas don't let go.

PEDRO. That's what they're trained to do. Fighting dogs don't let go. But you don't have to fight 'em. Mine was a good boy. Useta sleep together. I ain't ashamed. He was my friend. So when he got old, I wanted to be there for him. I just wanted to be there. So this one time he sorta arched his back like he was stretching and real slow he just sorta fell over. I was shouting "Come back! Come back boy!" but he wasn't breathing, his lips were blue. I never seen a dog turn blue. And all I could do was hold him and tell him to come back.... And he did. *(Silence.)* After that, the both of us kinda lived closer. So that, when he finally did ... die ... I cried, sure. But it wasn't outa fear. It was just for missing ... that closeness. That — *(Can't find the word.)* Whatever that thing is. *(Silence.)* Since then, I never really been that close to anybody. I never let myself. I never had the chance. Till now. *(Touches Garnet. After a moment, Garnet moves away.)*

GARNET. Why'd he come back?

PEDRO. He came 'cause I called him. I guess what I wanna know is — Can you get that close? Is it all right? I feel it — that stretching — I feel it coming on. Coming closer each day. And I don't have anybody. Nobody to call me back. *(Slight pause.)* What I wanna know is, if I should ever come to that — that thing, that place — who's gonna be there for me? Who's gonna call me? *(A moment, then.)*

GARNET. Pey-dro. *(Like calling a dog.)* Here, Peydro. *(Moving close.)* Here, Pedro.

PEDRO. Will you?

GARNET. Will you? *(Tenderly they come together, hold each other close. Slowly they kiss. At first it's brotherly, sweet. But more and more*

37

each man's desire takes over. Both are scared, both are hungry. Gar-
net takes off Pedro's shirt, then his own. They slowly go to their knees.
Up to this point, it's very romantic. Then, almost like rough trade,
both men start to grab and clutch. It's confusing, part turn-on, part
actual fight. It starts with a bite by Pedro, and leads to him hitting
Garnet. A trickle of blood comes from Garnet's split lip.)
PEDRO.   I'm sorry. I'm sorry.
GARNET.   *(Wiping the blood with his hand.)* That's all you know.
You poor dense muthafucka. You're just like your dog. But
you're not a dog. Time to sleep in your own bed.
PEDRO.   What?
GARNET.   Get outa here. *(We hear a dog barking. Drums. The*
gym. Mantequilla training slavishly, savagely. Alacran urging him
on with a new cocky attitude. Reporter interviews Vinal. Drums drown
out the words, but we can see him speak with his hands — colorful,
nasty. Then Pedro enters, hitting the mitts with Jack.)
JACK.   Jab, jab, jab — Here I come — That's it! — Now add
the hook! — To the body — Yeah! — Now finish him off — !!!
(Bell rings. Jack pulls off the mitts, but Pedro keeps punching the air
hard as he can, sweat pouring off him.) Hey. Enough already. *(No*
response.) Quit it now. What you tryna do, kill yourself? *(No re-*
sponse.) Jesus, kid — ! *(Throws his arms around him.)* What the
hell you doing?!!! *(Slaps him.)* WAKE UP!!!
PEDRO.   I'M AWAKE!!!
JACK.   Good! Shit. *(Winded.)* What you working so hard? Ain't
gonna have no fight left in ya! Now sit your ass down and
don't get up till I tell you, or you wanna see me mad? What
the hell is wrong with you — ?
PEDRO.   I can't tell y—
JACK.   Did I tell you to speak? Now you listen. You' the Man.
You don't got to prove nothing to nobody. Least of all me.
'Cause I think you're beautiful. Hell, I think you' the tail of
the dog. So don't be showing off to me. Save yer strength.
PEDRO.   Jack, I —
JACK.   Nuh! You save it. And *use* it. You' a fighter! All you
need to do is eat, and sleep, and dream good dreams. That's
all you need.
PEDRO.   I need to sweat this outa me.

JACK. This is life and death we're talking! *(Throws him a towel.)* Grab a shower. And cool yer damn heels. *(Stops him.)* I am here for you.

PEDRO. Are you?

JACK. 'Course I am. Dammit, you won the title for fighting, not fucking! Long as you defend your title like a man, — *(Breaks off.)* Sorry, son. I'm sorry.

PEDRO. Now I see. You are what you were before. Just everybody knows. *(Nearly crying.)* I thought the belt was supposed to protect me.

JACK. Naw. See, it's you got to protect the belt. *(Slight pause.)* What? Don't you want it no more? Hell, I'm half-dead and I still want that fucking belt. Shit, kid. You' the champ! We'd give our lives to be you. To be you. Don't that make you feel nothing? *(Pedro exits.)* What the fuck this world coming to? *(Sarita enters. Jack jumps up startled.)* What can I do for ya?

SARITA. I'm looking for Petey. *(No response.)* Petey. Pete Quinn.

JACK. You mean the champ?

SARITA. Petey to me.

JACK. *(Laughing.)* He'll be right back. *(Looking her over.)* Don't get too many women 'round here, 'cept of course the lady boxers. I seen a lady knock a fella down, not once but twice, right there in that ring.

SARITA. What? Supposed to let the guy win? *(Throws a blow.)* Spare me.

JACK. Say, you all right.

SARITA. I'm washed in the blood. My dad boxed.

JACK. Would I know him? *(She shakes her head.)* We boxers hang tight.

SARITA. Richie Lemos. *(Jack involuntarily rubs his nose.)* You knew him?

JACK. Only by reputation. Only by reputation.

SARITA. Dad like dogs. Petey raised 'em. Dad showed Petey how to box.

JACK. *(Snaps fingers.)* I knew I'd seen that style of his!

SARITA. Yep. He was a banger and a comer.

JACK. Like you. The thing your dad had is what the Spanish fighters call ma*chi*smo.

SARITA.   Ma*chi*smo.

JACK.   Yeah, that too. *(Pedro enters.)*

SARITA.   Hey.

PEDRO.   Hey.

JACK.   Hey! Well all right. I'll leave ya with the fine lady. *(To Sarita.)* Come around again, I'll tell ya a coupla stories about your dad. *(Exiting, to himself.)* Hot dog! I knew that boy flew straight! Thank you, Jesus.

PEDRO.   How's your dad?

SARITA.   Sick.

PEDRO.   Sorry.

SARITA.   Don't be, it's just tequila. The dog?

PEDRO.   Buried him.

SARITA.   Boy, that dog was a sex fiend. Remember, he used to —

PEDRO.   You remember that — ?

SARITA.   Prop up one leg and whack off with the other! Who could forget a thing like that? That was hot stuff! Who taught him that, I wonder?

PEDRO.   He's the one taught me.

SARITA.   Yeah, right. Remember that fight? That big black shepherd with the scars? Your boy was so dumb he tried to mount that killer dog! Geez. All that blood spurting out of your boy's head, but his tail was wagging! I guess he didn't feel it. Crazy.... So is it true? You know.... Queer? 'Cause I mean I been scouring my brain for clues, and it's not like you wore high heels or carried a purse or — *(Pedro motions for her to stop.)* So I'm nervous. But you wouldn't go out with me. And I wasn't bad then, was I?

PEDRO.   I don't go out with people.

SARITA.   You oughta try it sometime.

PEDRO.   I hurt people.

SARITA.   Love hurts people. Sometimes I feel just like your dog, trying to make love, and just getting bit. Just getting cut off. And like some stupid dog in heat coming back for more. Trying to feel that close, that —

PEDRO.   That feeling — that thing? It can't last.

40

SARITA. That's why you gotta grab it while you can. *(They are very close. Pedro leans in and kisses her. She kisses back. It gets passionate fast. Then each pulls away.)* No.

PEDRO. I can't.

SARITA. Whoa.

PEDRO. Sorry.

SARITA. Quit being sorry!

PEDRO. Well it's weird!

SARITA. Yeah, so?

PEDRO. So I want — *(Stops.)*

SARITA. What? *(He struggles.)* What do you want? Spit it out! *(Amazingly, with a freedom he has not shown before, Pedro does a Jackie Wilsonesque dance move.)* What was that?!!!

PEDRO. I dunno!!!

SARITA. I'd like to see you do that in the ring!

PEDRO. I wish I could. *(Pause.)*

SARITA. Your dog. When he killed that dog, he jumped straight in the air. I'll never forget that. Straight in the air. I better go find my man.

PEDRO. Me too. *(Gut bucket Rock 'n Roll. Club door opens. Garnet stands lighting up, smoking. Stained cummerbund, tie undone, hard-working man in show business. Then Pedro appears, out of breath, trying to smile.)* Hey. Been looking all over. *(Icy pause.)* Got your gig back. I thought you weren't gonna impers —

GARNET. Hey, we all impersonate. *(Snaps his fingers like nailing a move.)* And I'm pretty good at it too.

PEDRO. I'm sorry. I'm really sorry for what I done. But I'm back. I'll make it up to ya. And I wanna —

GARNET. Don't do that. Don't get close.

PEDRO. I'm not gonna hurt you —

GARNET. I'm not afraid of you or any man. I just don't wanna get bit.

PEDRO. I'm sorry —

GARNET. I'm about sick of hearing you say you're sorry. Sorry for what? For your dreams? Please. You ain't the first or the last to dream about another man. For what you done to me? I've been through worse. Be sorry for what you done to yourself. And what about you? You came to me, with your

41

sorry-ass dog story. And I was there for you. I was there. But you wouldn't go there. No, you'd rather take a royal ass-kicking. Let the Cuban kill you for your sins. For your dreams. Being sorry. As if that'll wash you clean. Make you the man. Got no clue, kid. Not a clue in the world. *(Slight pause.)* You know what I see when I watch a fight? I watch the men. Holding on as much hitting. And I see them in their corners getting massaged and Vaselined and whispered in their ear. I see the closeness. And I see the fear. The fear of what you can and cannot touch. No wonder they go out and try to kill each other. And then I see you. And then I really see. No wonder they cut you off. No wonder they want you dead. If you're their champ, then what the hell does that make them? *(Pedro goes to touch him.)* What are you gonna do, hit me?

PEDRO.   Come to the fight.

GARNET.   *(A realization.)* That's all you know. Grabbing and clutching and punching and kicking ass. That's love. Or the closest you've ever been.

PEDRO.   It is love.

GARNET.   It ain't l —

PEDRO.   It's my love.

GARNET.   Well it ain't mine. Look. Forget me. Forget all this. Get down to business. Don't be looking to nobody. And watch yerself in them clinches. That's what I forgot to do.

PEDRO.   Come to the fight. Please.

GARNET.   *(As music vamps from within.)* That's my set.

PEDRO.   Come to the fight!

GARNET.   Nope. You ain't gonna bite me twice. *(Adopts his performance attitude.)* Be who you are, man. Who you are. *(Intro music.)*

PEDRO.   Come back.

GARNET.   Gotta go. *(Pedro puts a hand out, but Garnet brushes past. A moment later we hear him singing a song like a James Brown song* to live accompaniment. But then he sees Pedro. Stops singing, drops the attitude, exits mid-song. Drums. The arena. An uneasy*

---

* See Special Note on Songs and Recordings on copyright page.

animal hum from the packed crowd. Ringside, hallways, dressing rooms. The principals assemble.)

TV REPORTER.   It's Decima versus Quinn, and the Garden is packed to the rafters! Good evening fans, and welcome —

VINAL.   *Oye nena!* Come on baby! *Dame* candy!

SARITA.   Please.

VINAL.   Wilfred Vinal, hundred sixty pounds of love. *Venga a verme.*

SARITA.   Listen, Wilfred, you're a walking catastrophe.

VINAL.   I could go blind dreaming of you. *(Drums. She rushes past him down the hall. Alacran stops her.)*

SARITA.   Let me see him.

ALACRAN.   See him after, *chula.*

SARITA.   I wanna see him now.

ALACRAN.   *Para que?*

SARITA.   None of your goddamn business.

ALACRAN.   It is my business.

SARITA.   *Hijo de la chingada!*

ALACRAN.   Nice mouth you got there. If you was my girl —

SARITA.   I'm not your girl. Please. I need to see him.

ALACRAN.   He told me to tell you. He'll see you after the fight.

SARITA.   That's a lie!

ALACRAN.   Sometimes, *chula,* a man's gotta get down to business. *(Congas.)*

TV REPORTER.   There's a circus atmosphere due to the Vinal allegations, not to mention a certain amount of bad blood between the two —

ALACRAN.   *(In the dressing room.) Que onda, chulo?*

MANTEQUILLA.   Where my girl?

ALACRAN.   How should I know? Prob'ly with some other guy — *(Mantequilla reacts, angry.)* Who the hell know?

MANTEQUILLA.   She no come?

ALACRAN.   She no come.

MANTEQUILLA.   You sure?

ALACRAN.   My business to be sure.

JACK.   *(In the other dressing room.)* Hey Champ. You okay? *(Pedro looks sick.)* Butterflies. Be all right once you're in there.

PEDRO.   Not butterflies. *(Drums.)*
VINAL.   *Oye mami,* you come back for me.
SARITA.   *Cabrón! (Takes a swing at him.)*
VINAL.   That's what I call a dream match. You and me baby!
SARITA.   Goddamn this whole *chingadera!*
VINAL.   *Munga munga,* baby! *(Drums.)*
MANTEQUILLA.   You sure she no come?
ALACRAN.   How many times I gotta tell you — ?
MANTEQUILLA.   She always come. *(Tears of rage.)* She always come.
ALACRAN.   Not always. *(Mantequilla swats the air viciously.)*
JACK.   Go throw some water on your face boy. Try to take a piss.
ALACRAN.   *Andele! Vamonos!*
JACK.   If you gotta throw up, do it now. When you come back, we gonna kick some ass! *(Drums. The urinal. Pedro spits up. Then Vinal enters.)*
PEDRO.   Exit's down the hall.
VINAL.   Who's going? I got business.
PEDRO.   Me too.
VINAL.   *(Looking him over.)* Not exactly god-like.
PEDRO.   Get away from me.
VINAL.   So you guys gonna fight or fuck? Betcha Mantequilla's getting some right now. That little bitch of his sucking on his candy. Don't worry. She'll take the edge off. Better he gets fucked. If he don't he's liable to kill your ass. But he's taken care of. So. How 'bout you?
PEDRO.   What?
VINAL.   'Cause hey, I came to see a fight. I can watch guys fuck anytime I want down by the docks — *(Pedro tries to exit, Vinal blocks him.)* But hey. Here's everybody getting fucked but you. Poor little Piccolo Pete. So I said to myself, why not come down and see the Man himself? Find out what he needs. God knows he needs some, and he sure as hell don't know how to get any on his own. So here I am. *(Kneels.)*
PEDRO.   Hey.
VINAL.   Come on. Take me. *(Kisses his belly.)* Go on. Take me.

44

PEDRO. What do you mean?

VINAL. What do you think? *(Starts to loosen Pedro's trunks.)*

PEDRO. What are you doing?

VINAL. *(Kissing.)* Letting you know. Who you are.

PEDRO. What?

VINAL. Who you are, man. Who you are.

PEDRO. What do you mean?!!! *(They grab and wrestle.)*

VINAL. Oh you like to clinch! Almost like the real thing — *(Yanks him close.)* Except it ain't.

PEDRO. Goddamn Rican bastard *puto* MARICÓN!!!

VINAL. I know who you are!!!

PEDRO. I'll fucking kill you!!!

VINAL. Everybody knows who you are!!!

PEDRO. I'll fucking kill you!!!! *(Jack enters.)*

VINAL. Now even you know who you are.

JACK. Get the fuck outa here. *(To Pedro.)* Time to go. *(As they exit, drums loud and furious.*

VINAL. *(Checks himself in the mirror.)* Put the blade to the heat. *(Drums. The ring like a pit. The fighters enter to massive cheers and jeers. Microphone drops from the rafters.)*

ANNOUNCER. Ladies and Gentlemen — Fifteen Rounds for the Undisputed Championship of the World —

SARITA. *Amorcito!!! (Mantequilla doesn't see her.)*

VINAL. Hey baby. You're sitting with the next champion of the world, soon as these two fuck each other to death —

SARITA. It'll never happen.

VINAL. Don't jinx me, baby —

SARITA. *(Staring right through him.)* Never. *(Buzzer, indicating ten-second warning. Drums. Mantequilla goes to one knee, genuflects. Bell rings. Round One. They touch gloves. The fight begins. We see the action as a series of snapshots, an accelerated fight punctuated by the drums. Punches land both ways.)*

JACK. *(From his corner.)* That's it!

ALACRAN. *(From his corner.)* *Como martillo!*

JACK. That's my boy — !

ALACRAN. Watch it now, watch it — !

VINAL. Wasn't nothing! *(Pedro lands hard. Mantequilla clinches. Pedro doesn't press the initiative. Bell rings.)* What the fuck was that?

JACK. *(As Pedro returns to his corner.)* Why you let him off the hook?

ALACRAN. *(As Mantequilla returns to his corner.)* Why you let him hit you like that?

VINAL. I could take both these guys on their best night.

ALACRAN. You need to do more!

JACK. Give me more! *(Buzzer.)*

REFEREE. Round Four! *(Bell. They fight. Pedro seems out of rhythm. Mantequilla scores well. Pedro seems to be getting hit flush on the chin.)*

ALACRAN. *En el hígado! El hígado! (Mantequilla staggers Pedro.) Que chulo!*

JACK. Aw hell! *(Bell rings. In the corners, Jack meets Pedro with a wet sponge, while Alacran applies Vaseline to Mantequilla's face.)*

MANTEQUILLA. Dyou see that?

ALACRAN. What?

MANTEQUILLA. He smiling at me!

ALACRAN. Another round like that, he ain't gonna have any teeth left to smile. Looking beautiful. *Como chocolate — !*

JACK. *(To an unresponsive Pedro.)* You okay? You okay?

SARITA. *(Trying to get close.)* Baby, you look beautiful!!! *(Buzzer.)*

REFEREE. Round Seven! *(Bell rings. Mantequilla flurries, then toys with Pedro, dancing and making him miss badly.)*

JACK. Hit him!

ALACRAN. *Múevete!*

VINAL. What is this, a first date?

ALACRAN. *Múevete!*

JACK. Hit him! *(Mantequilla lands a five-punch combination. Pedro doesn't fight back. Bell rings.)* What are you doing?

ALACRAN. Play with him!

JACK. What are you doing?

REFEREE. *(Coming over.)* Watch the heads!

JACK. Tell the other guy!!

ALACRAN. One thing — then do the other!

JACK. You think this is a game?

ALACRAN. Play with him!

JACK. This is a fucking dogfight!

REFEREE. Watch the heads.

ALACRAN. *Vete a la chingada, idiota!*

REFEREE. Just watch the heads!

JACK. You hear me? You hear me? *(Buzzer.)*

REFEREE. Seconds out!

JACK. My God, kid! You got it right there in the palm of your hand!

REFEREE. Round Eleven!

JACK. Chance of a lifetime — ! *(Bell rings.)* All our lives! We been waiting all our lives! *(The men fight viciously like dogs. Both are staggered. Again and again, they summon up their best. As the bell rings, each lands potentially his best shot. Neither goes down. The round over, Pedro grins, smiles all the way back to his corner.)*

MANTEQUILLA. He smiling at me!!!

ALACRAN. *Matelo!!!*

JACK. Kill the muthafucka!!!

SARITA. Just hold on!

VINAL. FAGS!!!!

REFEREE. *(Hearing Vinal.)* May be a fag, but he got a helluva left hook! *(Buzzer.)*

MANTEQUILLA. I go dead him.

REFEREE. Last Round. Touch gloves. *(Bell. Pedro offers his glove. Mantequilla punches him instead, then slams home the Suzie Q. Pedro staggers, badly hurt against the ropes. Mantequilla hammers him mercilessly. Pedro is hurt and staggering but he won't go down. Mantequilla, exhausted now, stops. Both of them are weak, spent. Alacran screams to get Mantequilla's attention.)*

ALACRAN. *TEATRO!!!!* *(Mantequilla leans in and kisses Pedro full on the lips. Freeze. Then he lands the Suzie Q with everything he has. Pedro goes down. Slow motion as drums beat out Pedro's heartbeat. He's on his knees, unable to focus. Mantequilla in the neutral corner, exhausted. Crowd on its feet, cheering wildly, full of bloodlust. Pedro looking around. Then he sees Garnet. Standing beside the empty seat in perfect suit and pompadour. He rises. Mantequilla's hand is hurt and he seems exhausted. Still he goes in for the kill. Hits him once, twice. Then Pedro slips the third, and in regular speed, connects with a monster shot. Now in vicious real time, Pedro punches*

Mantequilla over and over. Mantequilla's tangled on the ropes, he cannot go down. Pedro hits him again and again. Finally the Referee steps in. Mantequilla hangs lifeless. Pedro in ring center, like a pit bull, bathed in sweat, rejoices and jumps in the air. Flashbulbs freeze this moment in time. Crowd noise explodes. Then all sounds stop. Pedro, now able to focus, sees Mantequilla falling slowly to the canvas, half-smiling, dying. Pedro goes to him like a lover, takes him in his arms.)

PEDRO.   Come back. *(Garnet begins to sing, something hard and strong. Pedro kisses Mantequilla. The dog barks like crazy.)*

END OF PLAY

PROPERTY PLOT

Boxing bags
Jumping ropes
Boxing gloves (PEDRO, MANTEQUILLA)
Microphone
Cigarette (SARITA, GARNET)
Lighter or matches (SARITA, GARNET)
Wrapping for boxer's hands (MANTEQUILLA)
Championship belt (GARNET)
Drinking glasses
Toupee (REPORTER)
Jump rope (PEDRO, VINAL)
Gym bag (MANTEQUILLA)
Boxing mitts (PEDRO, JACK)
Wet sponge (JACK)
Vaseline (ALACRAN)

SOUND EFFECTS

Bull Terrier barking
Drums
Fight bell
Cheers, jeers, catcalls from crowd
Cheers, boos from a crowd
Crowd noise
Fight buzzer

TODAY'S HOTTEST NEW PLAYS

❑ **MOLLY SWEENEY by Brian Friel, Tony Award-Winning Author of** *Dancing at Lughnasa.* The told in the form of monologues by three related characters, *Molly Sweeney* is mellifluous, Irish storytelling at its dramatic best. Blind since birth, Molly recounts the effects of an eye operation that was intended to restore her sight but which has unexpected and tragic consequences. *"Brian Friel has been recognized as Ireland's greatest living playwright. Molly Sweeney confirms that Mr. Friel still writes like a dream. Rich with rapturous poetry and the music of rising and falling emotions...Rarely has Mr. Friel written with such intoxicating specificity about scents, colors and contours." - New York Times.* [2M, 1W]

❑ **SWINGING ON A STAR (The Johnny Burke Musical) by Michael Leeds. 1996 Tony Award Nominee for Best Musical.** The fabulous songs of Johnny Burke are perfectly represented here in a series of scenes jumping from a 1920s Chicago speakeasy to a World War II USO Show and on through the romantic high jinks of the Bob Hope/Bing Crosby "Road Movies." Musical numbers include such favorites as "Pennies from Heaven," "Misty," "Ain't It a Shame About Mame," "Like Someone in Love," and, of course, the Academy Award winning title song, "Swinging on a Star." *"A WINNER. YOU'LL HAVE A BALL!" - New York Post. "A dazzling, toe-tapping, finger-snapping delight!" - ABC Radio Network. "Johnny Burke wrote his songs with moonbeams!" - New York Times.* [3M, 4W]

❑ **THE MONOGAMIST by Christopher Kyle.** Infidelity and mid-life anxiety force a forty-something poet to reevaluate his 60s values in a late 80s world. *"THE BEST COMEDY OF THE SEASON. Trenchant, dark and jagged. Newcomer Christopher Kyle is a playwright whose social satire comes with a nasty, ripping edge - Molière by way of Joe Orton." - Variety. "By far the most stimulating playwright I've encountered in many a buffaloed moon." - New York Magazine. "Smart, funny, articulate and wisely touched with rue...the script radiates a bright, bold energy." - The Village Voice.* [2M, 3W]

❑ **DURANG/DURANG by Christopher Durang.** These cutting parodies of *The Glass Menagerie* and *A Lie of the Mind,* along with the other short plays in the collection, prove once and for all that Christopher Durang is our theater's unequivocal master of outrageous comedy. *"The fine art of parody has returned to theater in a production you can sink your teeth and mind into, while also laughing like an idiot." - New York Times. "If you need a break from serious drama, the place to go is Christopher Durang's silly, funny, over-the-top sketches." - TheatreWeek.* [3M, 4W, flexible casting]

DRAMATISTS PLAY SERVICE, INC.
440 Park Avenue South, New York, New York 10016 212-683-8960 Fax 212-213-1539

TODAY'S HOTTEST NEW PLAYS

☐ **THREE VIEWINGS by Jeffrey Hatcher.** Three comic-dramatic monologues, set in a midwestern funeral parlor, interweave as they explore the ways we grieve, remember, and move on. *"Finally, what we have been waiting for: a new, true, idiosyncratic voice in the theater. And don't tell me you hate monologues; you can't hate them more than I do. But these are much more: windows into the deep of each speaker's fascinating, paradoxical, unique soul, and windows out into a gallery of surrounding people, into hilarious and horrific coincidences and conjunctions, into the whole dirty but irresistible business of living in this damnable but spellbinding place we presume to call the world." - New York Magazine.* [1M, 2W]

☐ **HAVING OUR SAY by Emily Mann.** The Delany Sisters' Bestselling Memoir is now one of Broadway's Best-Loved Plays! Having lived over one hundred years apiece, Bessie and Sadie Delany have plenty to say, and their story is not simply African-American history or women's history...it is our history as a nation. *"The most provocative and entertaining family play to reach Broadway in a long time." - New York Times. "Fascinating, marvelous, moving and forceful." - Associated Press.* [2W]

☐ **THE YOUNG MAN FROM ATLANTA Winner of the 1995 Pulitzer Prize. by Horton Foote.** An older couple attempts to recover from the suicide death of their only son, but the menacing truth of why he died, and what a certain Young Man from Atlanta had to do with it, keeps them from the peace they so desperately need. *"Foote ladles on character and period nuances with a density unparalleled in any living playwright." - NY Newsday.* [5M, 4W]

☐ **SIMPATICO by Sam Shepard.** Years ago, two men organized a horse racing scam. Now, years later, the plot backfires against the ringleader when his partner decides to come out of hiding. *"Mr. Shepard writing at his distinctive, savage best." - New York Times.* [3M, 3W]

☐ **MOONLIGHT by Harold Pinter.** The love-hate relationship between a dying man and his family is the subject of Harold Pinter's first full-length play since *Betrayal*. *"Pinter works the language as a master pianist works the keyboard." - New York Post.* [4M, 2W, 1G]

☐ **SYLVIA by A.R. Gurney.** This romantic comedy, the funniest to come along in years, tells the story of a twenty-two year old marriage on the rocks, and of Sylvia, the dog who turns it all around. *"A delicious and dizzy new comedy." - New York Times. "FETCHING! I hope it runs longer than Cats!" - New York Daily News.* [2M, 2W]

DRAMATISTS PLAY SERVICE, INC.

440 Park Avenue South, New York, New York 10016 212-683-8960 Fax 212-213-1539